DEDICATION

To my best friend Justin - it's a privilege to share my
business, life, and love with you.
To my children Isaiah and Eli - your growth provides a constant
source of joy and pride.
To my cousin BJ – continue to fly high!

To my family, friends and future young readers.
Thank you for your support!

www.reallifelearning.ca

ELI'S 1ST WINTER CARNIVAL

BY: LISA BOWEN

ILLUSTRATED BY: NINA VANESSA PONTILLAS

Hi, my name is Elijah. But my friends call me Eli. Winter is my favourite time and today is the Winter Carnival. My big brother, Isaiah, has gone before. But this is my first time.

As I walk downstairs, my mother says, "It is as cold as ice cream outside."
So my brother and I put on our winter jackets.
Again, my mom said, "Don't forget to also put on your hat, scarves and gloves."

3

We all get dressed and my mom, my dad, my brother and
I set off through the woods to go to the Carnival.
Brrr! Outside is very cold. The hair inside my nose is freezing.
But I am so excited to be going to the Carnival.

"Look, Eli! There are some of our friends," Isaiah says.
They are having a snowball fight.
"Let's go," I shout as we run to join them.

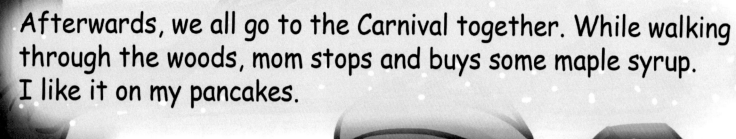

Afterwards, we all go to the Carnival together. While walking through the woods, mom stops and buys some maple syrup. I like it on my pancakes.

When I get to the Carnival, the first thing I want to do is to make snow angels. So my friend, Ben, and I quickly jump down into the snow and begin to wave our arms up and down.

Then it is time to play hockey. I like whizzing around on the ice.
My friend, Malakai, passes me the puck.
And guess what? I score a goal. Yippee!

Later on, Isaiah does ski jumping, flying high in the sky. I don't want anyone to know that I am too afraid of doing that.

So, instead, I go flying down the hill on a toboggan.
It's great!

After lunch, it is time for the snowman contest. The family who makes the wackiest snowman will win the prize. Our family wants to win!

We all pitch in. Dad and Isaiah make the body, mom makes the head and I do the hands and feet. Out of her bag, mom pulls an old red hat, a green scarf, a large carrot and some buttons for his eyes.

We quickly put them in place and we name our goofy looking snowman McSnowy. Then, we all line up beside our snowmen, waiting for the judges to decide which one is the wackiest. As the judges came by ours, I was so nervous I nearly fainted. Then they go back to the table.

One of them comes to the front and says," Well, the wackiest snowman is McSnowy."

I jumped up in the air and yell, "We won!"
Then I run and hug my mom and dad.
Isaiah goes and collects the prize.

We are all so happy. Malakai came across and said,
"Three cheers for Eli and his family!"
We all laugh.

As we walk back, I am smiling all the way. The snow keeps falling and by the time we get home, it is up to our knees.

Once inside, mom calls us for dinner. But guess what?
She serves us breakfast for dinner. But I don't mind.
I get to eat pancakes with fresh maple syrup. Yum! Yum!

After this, we gather around the fireplace drinking hot chocolate with marshmallows.

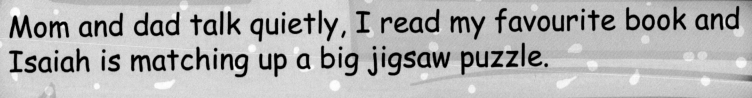

Mom and dad talk quietly, I read my favourite book and
Isaiah is matching up a big jigsaw puzzle.

22

I am getting very sleepy now. It's time for bed.
I go to my room, find my teddy bear and get into bed.
My eyes are closing fast. This has been a wonderful day.
I had a great time at the winter carnival and
I can hardly wait for the next one to come.
I fall asleep dreaming about it. ZZZZZ....zzzzzz

23

ABOUT THE AUTHOR

Lisa Bowen is based in Toronto; she's a writer, photographer,
publisher and a mother of two adventurous boys.
She is constantly amazed that she has any time to write,
but she doesn't sleep much. As a result, she can usually be
found with a green superfood smoothie in her hand.
Lisa believes that children should follow
their dreams and believe in themselves. It's through storytelling
she finds her footing in the world as a mom, spouse,
daughter, sister and a homeschool advocate.
Her future books include *Eli's Secret Pet*, *The Twins Go To School*,
New Baby Sisters, and *Eli & Max's Space Adventure*.

She is also the Co-Founder of Real Life Learning Inc.
Please follow her for more information at:
www.reallifelearning.ca
www.lisabowen.weebly.com
www.facebook.com/elis1stwintercarnival
Twitter: @eliswinterfun

Coming Soon

Over At Grandma's House

Story by: LISA BOWEN
Illustrations by: Nina Vanessa Pontillas

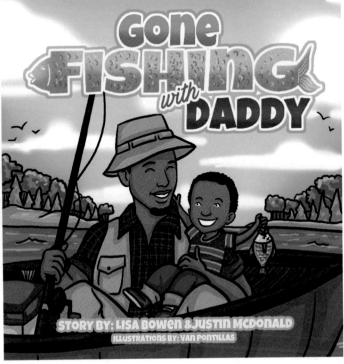

Gone FISHING with DADDY

STORY BY: LISA BOWEN & JUSTIN MCDONALD
ILLUSTRATIONS BY: VAN PONTILLAS

Prizes and Publication: The first-place winner will receive a book publication of his or her winning story. The second - and third-place winners will receive $50 each. Honourable mentions will also be awarded to entrants whose work demonstrates promise.

Stories must be original, unpublished fiction. Word count: 300 - 800.

Writers will be divided into 3 categories:
- Primary 6-9 years old
- Junior 10-12 years old
- Intermediate 13-16 years old

Writers of short fiction may now enter the 2017 Short Story Competition

Deadlines and Entry Fees: The entry fee is $25 USD for each story postmarked by May 31st, 2017.

To enter the contest, please visit www.lisabowen.weebly.com

RealLife Learning

Made in the USA
Middletown, DE
22 March 2017